Judy, Out of the Box

Lynn Woollacott

Judy, Out of the Box

First Edition 2020

Published by Dempsey & Windle
15 Rosetrees
Guildford
Surrey
GU1 2HS
UK
01483 571164
dempseyandwindle.com

British Library Cataloguing-in-Publication Data
A catalogue record for this book is available from the British Library.

ISBN: 978-1-913329-29-7

Acknowledgements:

Some of these poems have previously appeared in:
100 Vapour trails, Hedgehog Press;
50 Funny Poems for Children, Thynks publications;

Special thanks to Julia Webb and Helen Nelson for their advice and also The Norwich Stanza Group

Photographs by Lynn Woollacott

Previous Publications by Lynn Woollacott:

The Devil's Throat, *A Victorian Romance,* Amazon

Notes from the Balcony (2014) Indigo Dreams Publishing

Something and Nothing (2011) Indigo Dreams Publishing

Champion — Print, 1863

Foreword

The appearance of Punch and Judy shows originated in Italy, in the fourteenth century. An early poster depicts the first performance in London as witnessed by Samuel Pepys in 1662. The shows have been part of British culture in seaside towns, market towns and cities since then. In initial shows Punch would kill his wife and child; Ghost would appear, representing Judy and the ghost of Punch united together as one. Even today, Punch falls into hysterics every time he sees Ghost. Historically the Crocodile represented the Devil, and Shallabalah was the Grand Turk of Senoa. During the 1800's Shallabalah became the Publican.

Lynn's poems interact on Judy's co-dependant relationships. With dark and light shades in situations relevant to the characters this fictional world examines the human side of Judy's best and worst thoughts and behaviour.

Definition: A *swazzle* — a device held in the mouth of the Professor (the puppet master) to make the voice of Punch.

Contents

The Loyal Wife

shakes her head when he comes on stage
strokes his neck and says he's a good boy
is 'in the box' alone a lot
tells herself, *he'll come home soon*
rolls over on command
saves his favourite treats
is forever picking up his sausages
lets him walk in front of her
shuts out his *swazzle, swazzle, swazzle*
because occasionally he claims she is
the most beautiful girl in the world.

Sleeping Arrangements

Judy sleeps in an open box,
underneath her, Croc snaps,
Ghost moans,
Policeman raises his baton.

She worries for Baby
hums to soothe Baby,
tries to reach him with hollow hands.
Punch's nose pokes her face.

She'd do anything for a real house,
with an upstairs – a cot and a bed.
Doctor is whispering,

Put it this way, you'll never get
tonsillitis or appendicitis
never have arthritis in your knees
and though you think you do

you don't eat fish and chips,
cream cakes or iced buns
and your work will always cover the cost
of your living expenses.

Puppet masters will come and go
gazing into your face.
Never look in a mirror.
Never let him see what flows in your veins.

Judy dreams of flowery chaise longues
and blue velvet chesterfields.
She glides downstairs from Baby's room,
it's vast outside, a right royal garden
with giant chess pieces on the lawn.

That's the way we'll do it …
a little swazzle whispers in her ear.

Judy's Other Little Bit of Sweetness

Earlier today, Toby slithered on stage eager to get out for a small walk around, it still excites him. Sometimes (mostly) when it's dark in the box he rolls over and over everybody then he stands and balances on his paws, waiting for an instruction. He can't see or smell when it's dark and he's sleepy. I quickly put my hand out to comfort him and he wags his tail and slobbers.

Judy Sees a Little Bit of Pink

On the journey here the lid was off the box and the sky was like pink candy floss on a wide screen. We went over a high-pass road and an aeroplane soared right over us and shook the box. It made us laugh – even ghost *O'*ed.

Judy Hears Professor Padding on the Pier

He padded loudly as if his flip-flops stuck to the slats and he had to pull them up then shake them and his bare hairy toes; step by step he did this until he flapped back the curtain. Judy thought, *he's walked through yogurt, deep Greek yogurt, and purple grapes.*

Miss Polly is Distracted

How small this space is and how dark the panelling. The eight of us and Baby spend so much time down here, often with other guests. How small the battered brown suitcase is. There's a newspaper on the lid. A scent of printed matter mingles with a waft of salty sea.
Punch pops up-top after Judy. He dashes around – twists and shakes. He makes Toby dizzy spinning hoola-hoops from a string of sausages he stole from the pub. The children laugh and clap.
Over a century ago there was a tiny brown bottle of laudanum in the case, we used to inhale the fumes, loved its dizzying effects. These days even the fags have gone, but there's still a pong of after-shave warmed by summer heat – stifling in the darkened space.
What's taking Punch so long? It's a scene where we are supposed to be alone down here together. Judy's scolding only fuels his odd behaviour but she still carries on, sparked by her bad temper. I saw a book once called THINK POSITIVE, but it's out of our hands, we have no control over behaviour.
Punch is shouting, *Give me a kiss!* Something is flying through the air off stage. Judy screams, *Baby, BABY!* Ghost is rising …

Mind Readers on Stage

Judy holds up cards
in front of her face
crosses
circles
squares

his x-ray eyes
see nothing real   yet
he has *all* the answers

and oh those hearts
his so slow
and hers
so many times he stopped and restarted

she keeps her cards
silent and buried
underneath ghosts of the past

now she gets up and goes to
sit behind the curtain
to practise concentration.

Professor buys a pair of little shoes at an antique fair

Judy always preferred the colour pink
but these were crocodile shoes of the deepest green,

scaly, with a background hum of jungle
and small enough for a crow's feet.

They were made over a century ago.
She had lost them on the pier,

curiously drawn away by Monkey
who offered his audience a queen conch

with the ruse of listening to his homeland sea
while a pickpocket fishy as a carp

stole buttons off their shirts. Punch intervened,
aimed and bowled a brass ball across the pier slats.

Jester and Monkey rattled their fists and fled,
and Punch was – well – a hero.

But they had already stolen Judy's shoes
and the pink pearl buttons off her cardigan.

Oh the loss she had endured back then.
If she wore the shoes now, Croc

would surely thrash his tail and run towards
the tread of soft moccasin steps.

Laughter

Judy stood on stage when *gush*, a bucket of cold water fell over her. Joey ran up to her and fell over laughing. Toby barked and chased his tail. *What yer laughing at*? she yelled. Punch popped his head over and swazzled, *What yer expect, keep knocking on the door and running*? *What*? she cried back. *I just got here*. He laughed then and she knew he was just up to one of his tricks. Joey was still laughing and by now Toby was laughing. Punch kept going back for more buckets of water and throwing it over them and they made a game of dodging it. They laughed a lot afterwards. Judy went into the kitchen with Joey, he passed her a towel and went to make some toast. He asked Judy if she wanted some. She said no. Joey turned to get some sugar and Judy took the toast from his plate and took a big bite. Joey went to cook another bit of toast and Judy scoffed the rest of the first bit. Joey turned round with a tea towel and tenderly wiped Judy's chin. *Are you still wet, Judy?* he asked.

A Crocodile's Predicament

I was
content
and snappy
singing by the
muddy mire, intent
on a chilled out day,
so smug I thought,
Ha, you can't see me,
my camouflaged skin,
not even with binoculars
and zoom lenses. It was
obvious the cloud formations
predicted a stormy day unexpected when a tornado began to brew and howl.
It swirled and unzipped the jungle until it tore right through my pad.
I was a light, green kite
inside a howling, ghastly gale
which pulled my tail, and whoosh!
I landed in a suburban garden,
outraged and tangled in a tree. I
snapped, twisted and moaned,
It was the whipping wind that pushed and slapped, sucked
me up and threw me out like spitting fat from a sizzling sausage.
A little girl climbed the tree,
she untangled my frayed tail,
then lowered me gently and
said, *You creatures have*
peculiar features. Mind
your head! As I hit the
ground, she stared,
at that moment I
scarpered, I was
scared, hungry.
I ran on and on
spied a troop
of actors,
signed up,
miles
from
home.

Jumpers

On stage they leap onto pogo-sticks
bounce over chairs and the table,

they land, she's behind him,
then she springs in front of him,

he jumps an all-time high
bounces right over her shoulder.

She takes little joey-hops behind him
(but will never say sorry)

in fair competitiveness she knows
she can bounce back anytime

squash his silly pointy hat
and fill it with squishy trifle

and put it back on his silly pointy head.

Judy's Reflection

Judy plucks, plucks, plucks her top lip.
She creams, creams, creams her face
with lotions and potions.
She knows agony over and over
from gazing in the mirror.
She knows all about being stitched up.
She knows the shock horror expression
of an audience. She knows the difference
between those that can see her *real* self
and those that look straight through her.
She knows the needy, the spiteful,
the superior, the users and the pitiful.
Still, she gets by, does what she must
to keep a roof over Baby's head.

Judy's moody on the pier

Judy's happy to give up sausages,
fish and chips not so much, but Doc
said she can't eat like a hungry crocodile
anymore, she's slipping up.

She feels like an extra, her nose
is red from cold. She rarely sleeps –
in her nightmares she's a ghost
buried under a pile of puppets.

Punch has disappeared with Baby.
Policeman's gone to search
the red and white beach huts, asking after
a hooked-nose man with a swazzling voice.

Jack Ketch, with heavy gloves is rolling
a beer barrel towards the end of pier theatre,
she hunkers down in the shelter with Toby;
he licks her upside-down ice-cream.

Professor is looking down at the green sea
between the pier slats, one hand in his pocket,
she wonders if he's watching the scuttling crabs.
He enters his stripy kiosk, red curtain flapping.

She's waiting, aware she rarely makes
her own choices, she hears raised voices,
she knows that sometimes you have
to call it or put up and shut up.

Punch is shouting from a distance,
That's the way to do it. Disappear with Baby.
Strange, she thought that had been her plan.
She folds like a puppet with her dog

in a shelter.

Smokin' Puppets

Material crumbles from the singed hem of Judy's blue velvet cloak. *Salt doesn't help it,* Joey says. *Nor does jumping through flaming hoola-hoops on stage and spotting a flint stone painted with a red heart lying on the pier slats*, Judy thinks. Now she pukes at brown seaweed which stinks with each slush. Her cloak smells musty and smoky. She screws it up to make a pillow. Shallabalah's sticking his tongue out, he's no fire-eater, then he licks his lips of the crushed hawthorn berries Professor had rubbed them with. Everyone's dug deep in the box now except Punch, he's eating burnt sausages cooked in the flames. Judy tucks Baby's shawl tight. She hears a crab tapping on the outside of the box. Shallabalah's hypnosis skills blew her away tonight, he's mind-reading tomorrow. Punch is up. She knows she'll lose it and considers letting in the clawed one to see to him. *SHUT UP*, Shallabalah shouts. And they do.

Judy's nightmare at Shallaballah's poetry reading

Who was *she* wearing a Venetian white mask?
She followed me under the pier with witchy eyes.
I ducked under a door beam into the old-worldly
poet's den (a beach hut?!) and sat on a barrel.
She snuck in, her blonde plait spun and sparked
and cast a spell. It was pandemonium –

sea surged through the wood-wormed door,
ghostly figures started thrashing.
RUN RUN! shouted Shallaballah
to my cloaked grown-up baby son
(whose face I couldn't see).
The masked one watched on – unmoving.
I couldn't catch her with my stick.

I'm figuring it out, the other woman – though
I'm not supposed to (so it says in all the stories).
Was she a thief, a liar, a phantom phone-
caller, a stalker, a bully, or a husband stealer?
I fear over the centuries I've come to know
them all, except the last one. She wouldn't dare …

Judy's Teeth Chatter

Croc's drugged, jaw wide open.
Punch is pulling his teeth out,
he's nothing without his bite.

Croc's 69 teeth have turned into hatchlings,
thin green boys, gangly with tiny teeth.
They snap at the bottom of the box.

They wriggle up to Polly,
scurry up her sleeves, wrap around her neck.
Eyes glowing in the dark; they bother Judy.

Punch and Polly name all of them.
Whisper of their plans for them.
Judy thinks they're bonding.

Croc yawns and gum-snaps,
the hatchlings squirm and wriggle into his mouth –
a place where each of his teeth should be.

It's morning, a fluctus cloud waves
over the sea. Croc snaps the morning in.
Polly looks grey and broody.
Judy's teeth chatter.

Judy reflects on tinnitus

The past re-played out of the blue sometimes
catching Judy off guard. She saw herself

skipping under terrifying thunder clouds,
nev-er-safe-nev-er-safe. She remembered

the after-shock of running around the market
one-hundred times, a girl in a daze,

a flash of scurrying lizards, dead eyes
and squid tentacles dangling from balconies,

bells ringing in the white church steeple.
She watched for a witch or the devil in the dust

where she curled like a baby rat, the little rascals
running her neck, down her sleeves, and burrowing

under her rags. She smiled at them without
any upturn of her lips, in spite of the rotten fleas.

Didn't know back then of the choices she'd make,
didn't know of Trade Routes, or the Black Death,

didn't know of famine or Shallabalah's magic,
didn't know you could make the word

guilt out of guillotine.

Joey in the box

Hark, the click of Croc's teeth somewhere below.
Smell, hot dog. Feel, wet nose on my hand.
I sigh with pleasure in the box for the rustle
of petticoat, the scent of warm milk breath.
Judy's hand reaches down to check I'm still here.
I squeeze her fingers momentarily, smile inwardly, push
aside the bleak fog of 500 yesteryear – the way I talked
round the hangman much like Punch does now
(the way I taught him?) I have sausages, I shove one
in Croc's mouth as he surfaces from the bottom,
he snaps and sinks. Toby snuffles, I stroke his head.
Ghost moans at the commotion, I whistle an ancient
tune I sang in the alley and he listens,
I know he recognises it but he still can't piece together
the events of that night. Punch shivers above me.
Ghost quietens, Punch quietens.
We are all lifted off the floor, a sea breeze wafts in.
I sense fireworks from Judy; we all shiver in the box.

The Guilty One

(Enter Judy pushing Polly with her rolling pin. Polly is bound and gagged)

JUDY: 'Polly! Polly! You're for it now!'

(Forces Polly's neck under the guillotine)

JUDY: 'Phew it's hot. Are you hot? Oh I forgot you can't talk can you.'

POLLY: (Shaking and eyes pleading, doesn't make a sound.)

(Throw water (tears) onto midnight audience.)

JUDY: 'There's no-one there?'

(Bewildered, Judy looks out onto the empty pier, a drumbeat makes the sound of a rapid heartbeat.)

JUDY: 'I've always got 'The Palace Performance', even if Punch never married me. You've got no-one.'

(Pulls the lever to release the guillotine, it makes a loud thud.)

Polly's Head Falls

severed by [*the guillotine*]

falling onto [*the pier*]

mush
m
u
c
h
fuzziness
no
w
i
s
e
one
h
e
r
e
just
e
c
h
o
e
s
ghost lies beside, waiting

The Invisible Miss Polly

I
lady
became tangled up in potions
and smoke plumes
I
fairy
thought I could wave a magic wand
and grant my own wishes
I
insect
programmed to shrink smaller
A gust of wind came
uplifted me away
I
exist somewhere
voiceless

Judy's caught up in a crab line

On the pier a headless ghost
points to the white rails. Above the windows
of the closed café dew-kissed billboards tell
of shows to come. Judy knows she should pick
Polly's head up from the wooden slats, but
she glances with glass eyes at a slither of squid
on a tangled crab line wrapped around a post.
Grey sea slops flint stones to the shore,
sifts the lighter ones for amber. Sunrise
turns the sea blood-orange. A seal leaps
out of the water, wriggles onto a sandbank,
roly-poly's his blubbery self back into splash,
he's all sparkles and stars, he rolls
out and repeats his game several times. Judy
wonders if he can see the colour orange.
Professor's footsteps rattle the boards, he's
whistling, head down, hands in his pockets.
She knows she should move but she's lost
all sensation. The sea turns pale blue,
the seal dives under waves and vanishes.

Note to Hand-finisher

Re Polly

Fix scraggy neck so clothes can fit snug

Make a new (silk) (to fit largish hand) undergarment

Make a fancy new pink outer-gown

Give her face a new paint, especially her eyes (a new lustre?) she has to speak with her eyes

The ticking clock

Polly has been rushed somewhere with no head.
        He doesn't know who did it.

        A Shallaballah's magic trick special?

There's a pile of sweets on the sideboard
but he's locked the gates and turned
the outside light off. Something's up …

        She wished Joey was nearby.

She's sat against a book on the edge of Professor's desk.
She wants to go home.

That's the way to do it, Professor says
through gritted teeth just before the sound of

        the doorbell
        and several ghosts.

Professor on the Door Incident

In 2016 they found evidence of gravitational waves and proof of black holes. Punch and I knew the hypothesis was true long before this because he and Judy have always been pulled towards each other and then repelled by each other and then it's like she's in one black hole and he's in another. They say all the discovered waves will allow them to study other things, the floating about in space things, the solitary things that go their own way. They are apart now. I know I pushed things too far by making her behead Polly. And then in the morning Punch & Judy had to go on stage and perform the door incident.

I pushed the door open on stage and wondered if just once he'd let Judy pass. But no, Punch just kept pushing back. So they were wedged in the doorway for ages. My shoulders hurt! He didn't even look at Judy, but kept swazzling to the audience. Eventually she stopped pushing and he went without looking back. She fell on the stage floor weeping. Croc came up and jumped right over her, followed by Policeman, Jack Ketch and Doctor. A black hole formed in the pit of my stomach while everyone was laughing at Punch hiding sausages in Baby's shawl. All I could see was the swirling black hole Judy was in because I couldn't get her up. Judy couldn't get up and then Joey came and pulled her down into the box and he went off to rescue Baby. In the box Judy would hear Baby crying and a lot of shouting going on up top.

Judy has a proper day off

Judy drifts
like cotton-wool puffs
hunting down lost horse-shoes
on the beach. She watches reflections
in pools of cormorants wing-drying
on wooden groynes. She counts
the time it takes for beadlet-anemones
to slide from the tip of a flint rock
to the base (under water).
She sings like an alto-cumulus
while stone picking for dinosaur teeth
on the shingle beach. She walks
the strand line for feathers
to make dream-catchers. She learns
warm westerly breezes. She waves
a lot, paddles a lot, and makes tea
in the beach hut where diamond-
dust settles on sea-shells.

The Main Cast Interview

In three short sentences tell me what you are grateful for.
(Professor, the puppet master)

For myself
For my intelligence
For always being right
Punch

For dreams
For Baby
For love *Judy*

For my resurrection
That I can't actually physically get hold of anyone
That the others tolerate me
Ghost

What you asking me for? *(Looks up to the left for a minute)*
For my disguise
That I'm easily distracted
Jack Ketch
(the hangman)

For just being here
For being close to those I love
For work of course

Joey / clown

Flutters her eyes as if to say
My beautiful eyes
Holds her palms open and looks around as if to say
My beautiful friends (*a wary glance in Judy's direction*)
Holds her dress out as if to say
My beautiful new pink silk dress

Polly

For sausages
For sausages
Okay sausages

Toby the dog

Bibliography

Labour London and the London Poor Volume III, Henry Mayhew, pages 43 - 55, Cosimo Classics.

www.punchandjudy.com